ADELE

SOULFUL SINGER

HEATHER E. SCHWARTZ

Lerner Publications
MINNEAPOLIS

Lerner Publications Company
A division of Lerner Publishing Group, Inc.
241 First Avenue North
Minneapolis, MN 55401 USA

For reading levels and more information, look up this title at
www.lernerbooks.com.

Library of Congress Cataloging-in-Publication Data

Schwartz, Heather E., author
    Adele : soulful singer / by Heather E. Schwartz.
        pages   cm. — (Pop culture bios)
    Includes index.
    ISBN 978-1-4677-5718-8 (lib. bdg. : alk. paper)
    ISBN 978-1-4677-6101-7 (pbk.)
    ISBN 978-1-4677-6321-9 (EB pdf)
    1. Adele, 1988-—Juvenile literature. 2. Singers—England—
Biography—Juvenile literature. I. Title.
ML3930.A165S39 2015
782.42164092—dc23 [B]   2014028740

Manufactured in the United States of America
1 – PC – 12/31/14

INTRODUCTION

Adele performs at the
Brit Awards in 2012.

Adele was about as far from her roots as she could be. Not long ago, she'd lived with her mother in a small apartment above a discount store. Now, in December 2013, she was dressed to the nines in England's Buckingham Palace. Wearing a designer gown, Adele had accessorized to show her own signature style. Her beehive hairdo was topped with a veil. Her manicured nails featured jeweled crowns.

Adele holds a special award she recieved at Buckingham Palace in 2013.

Adele looked every bit the part of a polished young aristocrat. But she couldn't stifle her larger-than-life personality for long.

When her name was announced in the ballroom, Adele's smile stretched into a grin. She walked to Prince Charles, who pinned an MBE award to her dress. The award made her a Member of the Most Excellent Order of the British Empire for services to music. After receiving her award, Adele chatted with Prince Charles and shook his hand. Before leaving, she curtsied politely.

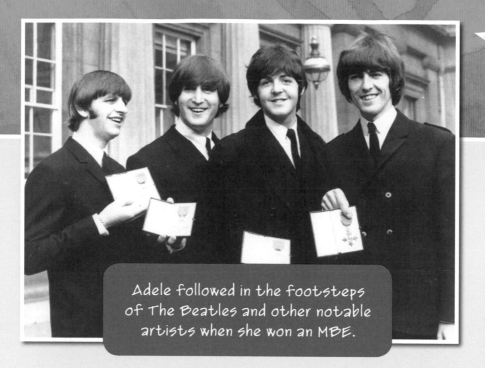

Adele followed in the footsteps of The Beatles and other notable artists when she won an MBE.

As she walked away, though, Adele couldn't help herself. She started to laugh. It seemed she couldn't believe what had just happened. She had grown up in a humble home in South London. Now she was an international singing sensation who'd just shaken hands with an actual prince!

In spite of her laughter, Adele was well aware that the honor she'd received was no joke. She was thrilled to be recognized by her country's royal family. And she was in very good company in winning her award. Many notable actors, authors, and artists had received awards at Buckingham Palace on that same day.

"It was an honor to be recognized...alongside such wonderful and inspirational people," she said afterward. **"Very posh indeed."**

Adele has come a long way from her humble beginnings.

CHAPTER ONE

REGULAR ROOTS

Adele moved to Brixton when she was eleven years old.

Musical talent doesn't run in Adele's family. But creativity does. Her mother was an art student when Adele was born.

Adele wasn't always known to the world by just one name. When she was born on May 5, 1988, she was Adele Laurie Blue Adkins. Growing up in England, she lived with her mother. The family of two was poor and moved around a lot. But Adele enjoyed the adventure of starting new schools.

Adele has had a passion for playing the guitar since she was a young girl.

As a young student, Adele learned to play the guitar and the clarinet. She also loved singing and performing for her mom and friends. By high school, it was clear she didn't belong in a regular public school. She belonged in a school for performers.

AUDITION =
to try out for an opportunity in the performing arts

Life-Altering Audition

At fourteen years old, Adele auditioned for the Brit School for Performing Arts and Technology and got in. That meant she was following in the footsteps of other students who'd already made it as performers, such as Amy Winehouse and Jessie J.

Just like Adele, Amy Winehouse attended the Brit School for Performing Arts.

Around the same time, Adele discovered a new source of inspiration. Shopping in a music store, she found jazz and blues albums by Etta James and Ella Fitzgerald. Their sound was different—and Adele loved it. She worked to train her own voice to sound soulful and passionate like them.

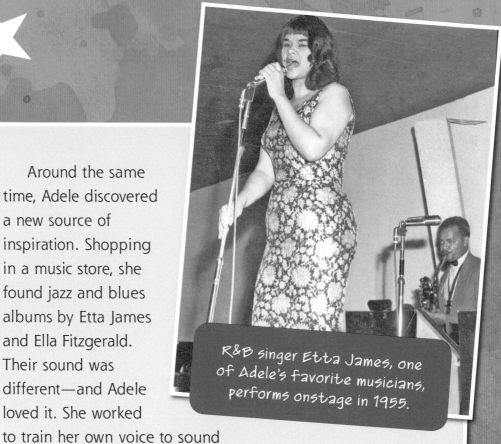

R&B singer Etta James, one of Adele's favorite musicians, performs onstage in 1955.

Out-of-Step Student

Adele loved being a student at the Brit School. She had time to write songs and play guitar. But Adele wasn't always the best student. She sometimes arrived at school four hours late. She once overslept and missed an important class trip. She was almost expelled.

Although Adele wasn't always on time, she was learning a lot at her new school. Teachers and classmates could see she had talent. During her second year of school, her classmate Shingai Shoniwa moved into an apartment near Adele's in South London. Shingai was a singer like Adele. Adele heard her songs and felt inspired. She wanted to write her own music too.

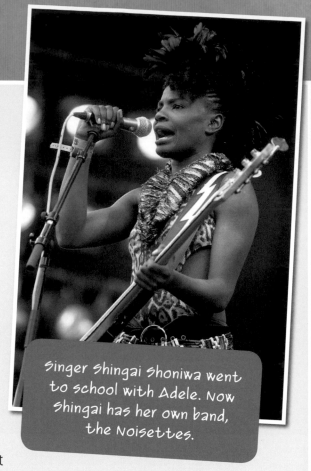

Singer Shingai Shoniwa went to school with Adele. Now Shingai has her own band, the Noisettes.

In 2006, Adele's last year of school, she recorded a three-song demo for one of her classes. The demo impressed her friends. One friend posted it on a MySpace page he had made for Adele in 2004.

DEMO =
a short recording that demonstrates a singer's style and abilities

Unbelievable Offers

Adele's MySpace page featuring her music was two years old by then. It wasn't incredibly popular. But once the demo was posted, her page suddenly got loads of attention. Adele had never really believed she could be a big star. So when important people in the music industry tried to contact her by e-mail, she ignored them. She thought they couldn't possibly be who they said they were.

Finally, Adele's mother convinced her to take the e-mails seriously. Adele accepted a meeting with XL Recordings, an independent record label. She never thought they'd sign her. But they did.

Just a few months after graduating from high school, eighteen-year-old Adele was preparing to launch her singing career.

MUSICAL INSPIRATION

Adele's musical influences include Destiny's Child, Mary J. Blige, Aretha Franklin, and Marvin Gaye.

CHAPTER TWO

STAR ON THE RISE

Adele performs in Brighton, England, in 2007.

As a newly professional singer, Adele found work quickly. She performed in restaurants and on TV. She sang with singer Jack Peñate on his first album, *Matinée*. She also began working on original songs. She wrote her first single, "Hometown Glory," in just ten minutes.

The song held a personal message for her mother. In the song, Adele explained why she wanted to stay in London rather than leave for college. She shared her message with the public when she released the single in October 2007.

TV STAR

Adele's song "Hometown Glory" was featured on the 2008 season finale of the TV show *Grey's Anatomy*.

SINGLE = a recording of just one song

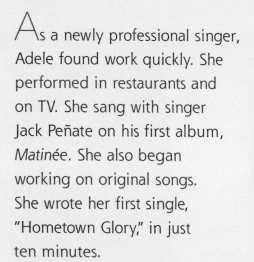

Starter to Star

Filling an album with brand-new songs was Adele's next challenge. But she had plenty of personal material to draw from. She'd recently fallen in love and then had her heart broken. She used her heartbreak to write many new songs. In January 2008, she released her debut album. It was named *19* because she was nineteen years old when she wrote the album.

Later that year, Adele was asked to perform on the TV show *Saturday Night Live*. She sang songs from her album, including "Chasing Pavements." An audience of more than 14 million people watched, listened, and loved her sound.

Overnight, her popularity skyrocketed. Adele was suddenly a huge star.

TOPPING ITUNES

Before Adele performed on *Saturday Night Live* in 2008, her album was at No. 40 on iTunes. The next day, it hit No. 1.

Award-Winning Artist

In 2009, Adele earned four Grammy Award nominations. She told the media she was more interested in a solid career than in any award. But when she won Best New Artist and Best Female Pop Vocal Performance, she couldn't hide her excitement.

Looking amazed, she made her way to the stage. She named the many people who'd helped her along the way. **"Thank you so much,"** she said. **"I'm gonna cry."**

Enduring Talent

Adele had hit a high point in her career. But she was far from finished. She began working on her second album. Adele used her feelings and experiences to come up with ideas for new songs.

Adele holds her Grammy Award for Best New Artist.

And Adele had plenty of strong feelings. That's because, at the age of twenty-one, Adele was in love again. Her new boyfriend inspired her to travel, read, and write poetry—and, of course, music.

But then, things took an unfortunate turn for Adele.

AND THE WINNER IS...

Judges at the 2008 Brit Awards could see Adele was a singer with major star potential. They honored her with the first-ever Critics' Choice Award.

Like her former relationship, this romance wasn't meant to last. She and her boyfriend broke things off. Adele's heart was crushed.

After the breakup, Adele sometimes found herself in tears at the studio. But, as always, she poured her feelings into her work. Her passion paid off when she released her second album to great acclaim.

PET PROJECTS

Adele has a dachshund named Louis Armstrong, after the singer. She has talked about getting another dog and naming it after Ella Fitzgerald.

Adele performs songs from her album 21 in London in 2011.

CHAPTER THREE

SINGING SENSATION

Adele poses at the 2011 MTV Video Music Awards.

ALTER EGO =
a character that a performer pretends to be onstage

Adele spent much of 2011 touring to promote her new album. She didn't especially enjoy it. She was too stressed. She worried tons about putting on a good show. She didn't ever want to disappoint her audiences. Sometimes, her anxiety about performing even made her sick.

Still, she was a professional. And she loved singing. So she figured out ways to overcome her stage fright. She calmed her nerves by cracking jokes. She also imagined herself as someone else onstage. Adele's alter ego was Sasha Carter, a fearless combo of country singer June Carter and Beyoncé's alter ego, Sasha Fierce.

STARSTRUCK

Adele freaked out when she met Beyoncé (FAR RIGHT). She was shocked to learn Beyoncé was one of her fans.

Sidelined Singer

Later that year, Adele had to cancel several shows. She needed vocal cord surgery that couldn't wait. Though performing live wasn't easy, Adele was devastated.

"Singing is literally my life," she wrote to fans on her website. "It's my hobby, my love, my freedom, and, now, my job. I have absolutely no choice but to recuperate properly and fully, or I risk damaging my voice forever." She went on to promise, **"I will be back, and I'm gonna smash the ball out the park once [I am]."**

Adele holds one of the many awards she's received in this photo taken just before her vocal cord surgery.

Adele's album *21* set a Guinness World Record in 2012. It was the first album in the United Kingdom to sell three million copies in one year.

Back on Track

Adele kept her promise to her fans. In February 2012, she performed "Rolling in the Deep" from her album *21* at the Grammy Awards. She really did smash the ball out of the park! When she finished, audience members stood to applaud.

Adele amazed the crowd with her performance at the 2012 Grammy Awards.

At the end of the night, Adele had six more Grammys to take home. A few months later, she announced that she was working on a third album. Since she wanted to write all the songs herself, it would be a while before it was ready for release. But she promised fans a new single soon.

Adele proudly displays
her six Grammys.

Adele with fiancé Simon Konecki in 2012.

Meanwhile, Adele's personal life was falling into place too. While recovering from surgery, she'd met a new boyfriend, Simon Konecki. By the summer of 2012, they were engaged.

CELEBRITY STYLES

Adele names the wigs she uses to create her signature big-hair look. She has one named after singer June Carter and another named for writer Jackie Collins.

A Star's Bright Future

In October 2012, Adele released "Skyfall," the theme song for a new James Bond film. She also gave birth to a child, a boy she and Simon named Angelo.

As a new mother, Adele stayed out of the spotlight. In January 2013, however, she went to the Golden Globe Awards. When she won a Golden Globe for "Skyfall" —and an Oscar Award one month later—she was back big time. And she had plenty of plans for her future.

In 2014, Adele announced that her third album was nearly ready for release. She even set tour dates for 2015. A performer through and through, she was set to focus on singing again. Her millions of fans were psyched to welcome her back.

KIND SOUL

In March 2014, Adele used her fame to gain support for her fiancé's charity work. His organization, Drop4Drop, provides access to clean drinking water. Adele tapped Twitter to encourage fans to get involved.

Adele performs at the Brit Awards in 2012.

ADELE
PICS!

Adele attends the Brit Awards.

Adele performs in
Germany in 2011.

SOURCE NOTES

7   Owen Tonks, "Adele Awarded MBE by Prince Charles and Calls Her Trip to Buckingham Palace 'Very Posh Indeed,'" *Mirror*, December 19, 2013, http://www.mirror.co.uk/3am /celebrity-news/adele-awarded-mbe-prince-charles-2943705.

17   "2009 GRAMMY Awards—Adele Wins Best New Artist," YouTube video, 1:52, from the 51st Grammy Awards televised by CBS on February 8, 2009, posted by "CBS," February 11, 2009, https://www.youtube.com/watch?v=9ZAFxGAaj7c.

22   Adele Adkins, "Important Blog," *Adele* (blog), October 4, 2011, http://www.adele.tv /blog/352/important-blog.

MORE ADELE INFO

Adele on Facebook
https://www.facebook.com/adele
See pics and find out what Adele's up to.

Adele on Twitter
https://twitter.com/OfficialAdele
Keep up with Adele on the road.

Adele's Official Site
http://www.adele.tv
Read Adele's blog and get the latest news on this sensational singer.

Doeden, Matt. *Adele: Soul Music's Magical Voice.* Minneapolis: Twenty-First Century Books, 2013. Read more about Adele's journey from London girl to megastar.

James, Sarah-Louise. *Adele: A Celebration of an Icon and Her Music.* London: Carlton Books, 2012. Learn more about Adele as a singer and musician.

Shapiro, Marc. *Adele: The Biography.* New York: St. Martin's Griffin, 2012. Read up on Adele's rise to fame.

INDEX

The images in this book are used with the permission of: © Steve Granitz/WireImage/Getty Images, pp. 2, 24; © Andy Sheppard/Redferns/Getty Images, pp. 3 (top), 20 (top); © Jon Kopaloff/FilmMagic/Getty Images, pp. 3 (bottom), 28 (right); © Jeff Kravitz/Getty Images, p. 4 (top left); © Dave M. Bennett/Getty Images, pp. 4 (top right), 10; © Dave J Hogan/Getty Images, p. 4 (bottom), 14 (top right), 22; © John Stillwell/WPA Pool/Getty Images, p. 5; Brady Jonathan/PA Photos/ABACA/Newscom, p. 6; AP Photo, p. 7; ©Gareth Davies/Getty Images, p. 8 (top); © Alistair Laming/Alamy, p. 8 (bottom); © Gregg DeGuire/FilmMagic, p. 9; © Michael Ochs Archives/Getty Images, p. 11; © Greetsia Tent/WireImage/Getty Images, p. 12; © Dave Etheridge-Barnes/Getty Images, p. 14 (bottom left); Andre Csillag/Rex USA, p. 15; © Tim Mosenfelder/Getty Images, p. 16; © Robyn Beck/AFP/Getty Images, p. 17; © Studio 101/Alamy, p. 18; © Tom Oxley/The Hell Gate/CORBIS, p. 19; © Sean Gallup/Getty Images, p. 20 (bottom left); © Christopher Polk/Getty Images, p. 20 (bottom right); © Larry Busacca/WireImage/Getty Images, p. 21; © Kevin Mazur/WireImage/Getty Images, p. 23, 28 (top middle); AP Photo/Rex Features, p. 25; © Josiah W/Spash News/CORBIS, p. 26 (top); © Paul Drinkwater/NBC Universal/Getty Images, p. 26 (bottom); © Mike Marsland/WireImage/Getty Images, p. 27; © Eamonn McCormack/WireImage/Getty Images, p. 28 (bottom); © Jon Furniss/WireImage/Getty Images, p. 28 (top left); © Stefan M. Prager/Redferns/Getty Images, p. 29 (bottom left); © DFree/Shutterstock.com, p. 29 (top left).

Front cover: © Jason Merrit/Getty Images, (large image); © DFree/Shutterstock.com, (small image).

Back cover: © WPA Pool/Getty Images.

Main body text set in Shannon Std Book 12/18.
Typeface provided by Monotype Typography.